For Your Baby's Baptism

Selected by

Peter Dainty

kevin mayhew

The Parents' Prayer

Father,
   today you welcome our baby
   into the life of your Son.

With Christ and in Christ
   may our child be filled with your glory.

Let him hear
   in his heart
   your words:
   'This is my child,
   my beloved child.'

When times are good,
   may he turn to you.

When times are hard,
   may he turn to you.

And always,
   may he be
   a channel of your peace.

F Mary Callan

Jesus, may ...(name)... grow in
    knowledge and love of you each day.
May every step of his life
    be walked along your way.
Watch over him and guide him
    to know you as his Lord and Saviour.

Heavenly Father, give ...(name)...
    a deep love of learning,
    and the wisdom to understand
    how to use the knowledge he gains.
May he know the joy of curiosity
    and wonder in your beautiful world.
May he never stop asking questions.

Lord of all, bless ...(name)... with a
   deep sense of joy and happiness
   throughout his life.
When times are hard –
   as sometimes they will be –
   may he still have a thankful heart
   for blessings received,
   and for your faithful presence.
Amen.

Susan Hardwick

Jesus, may ...(name)... always know
    the joys of loving and being loved.
May she never know
    what it is to be lonely.
May she be generous
    and compassionate
    and quick to understand and respond
    to the needs of others.
May the world be a better place
    for her presence in it.
Amen.

Susan Hardwick

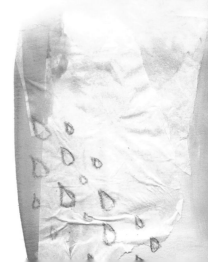

God of all, guide ...(name)...
   along the path of life
   you have chosen for her.
May she greet each bright new day
   with joy and excitement
   at all that it might bring.
May she always
   be filled with wonder.
May she always
   walk with you.
Amen.

Susan Hardwick

A Godparent's Prayer

Jesus, on ...(name)...'s special day
  there's so much I want to pray for.
My heart is brimming over with wishes,
  hopes and dreams for him
May those that are right for him
  come true.

I'm filled with awe at what it means
  to be his godparent.
Help me to do it as you would want.
Help me to be faithful
  to the promises I shall make.

Jesus, guide me
    through the days and years
    in my relationship with ...(name)...
May I always be sensitive
    to his needs.

Give me the wisdom, insight
    and awareness
    to know what attitude
    and behaviour
    is appropriate and right.
May all that I do and say
    be pleasing to you.

Susan Hardwick

As the falling raindrops
   make the trees and flowers grow,
   may the water of baptism
   help this little one
   to blossom in spirit,
   in grace
   and in understanding.
In the name of Jesus Christ.
Amen.

Peter Dainty

,Sprinkle down upon her
   your grace.
Give to her
   virtue and growth.
Give to her
   strength and guidance.
Give to her
   flocks and possessions,
   sense and reason void of guile;
   that she may stand
   without reproach
   in your presence.

See Israel's gentle Shepherd stand
  with all-engaging charms.
Hark how he calls the tender lambs,
  and folds them in his arms.

'Permit them to approach,' he cries,
  'nor scorn their humble name.
For 'twas to bless such souls as these
  the Lord of angels came.'

We bring them, Lord, in thankful hands,
  and yield them up to thee.
Joyful that we ourselves are thine,
  thine let our children be.

Philip Doddridge (1702-51)

The Lord bless you and keep you.
The Lord smile upon you,
   and be kind to you.
The Lord look with favour upon you,
   and give you peace.

Numbers 6:24-25

A Parent's Prayer

Loving Father,
  you know how hard
  life in this world can be.
My instinct is to want to protect
  my daughter from every hardship.
Yet I know this cannot be –
  sickness, accidents, troubles,
  pain, trials, sadness
  and ultimately death
  are unavoidable.
But I ask that I may
  always be there for her
  to protect when I can,
  especially in the early years,
  and also to help, guide
  and encourage
  through the hard times.

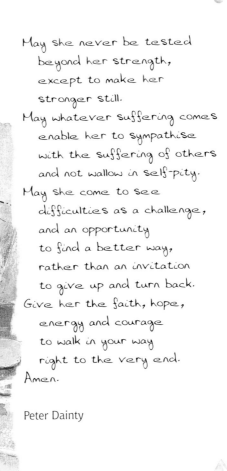

May she never be tested
   beyond her strength,
   except to make her
   stronger still.
May whatever suffering comes
   enable her to sympathise
   with the suffering of others
   and not wallow in self-pity.
May she come to see
   difficulties as a challenge,
   and an opportunity
   to find a better way,
   rather than an invitation
   to give up and turn back.
Give her the faith, hope,
   energy and courage
   to walk in your way
   right to the very end.
Amen.

Peter Dainty

Almighty God
   and heavenly Father,
   we thank you for the children
   which you have given to us.
Give us also grace to bring them up
   in your faith, reverence and love,
   that as they advance in years,
   they may grow in grace,
   and be found in the number
   of your own family;
   through Jesus Christ our Lord.
Amen.

John Cosin (1595-1672)

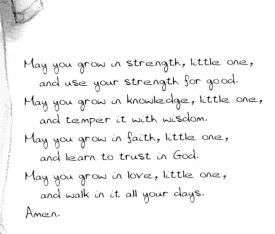

May you grow in strength, little one,
    and use your strength for good.
May you grow in knowledge, little one,
    and temper it with wisdom.
May you grow in faith, little one,
    and learn to trust in God.
May you grow in love, little one,
    and walk in it all your days.
Amen.

Peter Dainty

17

Lord, we bring our child
   to this holy font,
   that he may be
   cleansed and strengthened
   by the refreshing power
   of your Holy Spirit –
   the Water of Life –
   both now,
   and all his days.

Lord, we bring ourselves
   to this holy font,
   that we may be
   cleansed and strengthened
   by the refreshing power
   of your Holy Spirit –
   the Water of Life –
   and be equipped
   to care for ...(name)...
   and teach him your ways.
Amen.

Peter Dainty

It fell upon a summer day,
    when Jesus walked in Galilee,
    the mothers from the village brought
    their children to his knee.

He took them in his arms, and laid
    his hands on each remembered head.
'Suffer these little ones to come
    to me,' he gently said.

'Forbid them not. Unless you bear
    the childlike heart your hearts within,
    unto my kingdom you may come,
    but may not enter in.'

Then, Jesus, look upon this child
    that he may come to you and feel
    your hands on him in blessing laid,
    love-giving, strong to heal.

Stopford Augustus Brooke (1832-1916)

The Baby's Prayer

Though I may be very small
  and all around me big and tall,
  Abba, Father, you are near,
  so I have no need to fear.

Though I have no words to say,
  you will teach me day to day.
There are thoughts within my mind,
  which sense what's good
  and know who's kind.

As I sleep, and play, and feed,
  you remind me what I need:
  just one word from heaven above,
  and that word is simply – Love.
Amen.

Peter Dainty

An Infant's Prayer

Lamb of God, I look to thee;
   thou shalt my example be.
Thou art gentle, meek, and mild;
   thou wast once a little child.

Thou didst live to God alone;
   thou didst never seek thine own.
Thou thyself didst never please:
   God was all thy happiness.

Loving Jesus, gentle Lamb,
 in thy gracious hands I am.
Make me, Saviour, what thou art;
 live thyself within my heart.

I shall then show forth thy praise,
 serve thee all my happy days.
Then the world shall always see
 Christ, the holy child, in me.

Charles Wesley (1707-88)

An Older Brother or Sister's Prayer

Father, thank you for my baby brother.
He seems so small
  and knows so little,
  so he needs all the love
  we can give him.
I can't remember being christened,
  and I don't suppose he will either,
  but it's good to know that
  you loved us and
  welcomed us into your family
  even before we were aware of it.

Help me to love ...(name)...
   and look after him
   like a big brother should –
   not be jealous
   when he seems to get
   more than his fair share of attention;
   not be impatient with him
   when he's being a pain
   and won't leave me alone;
   but help and encourage him
   when he tries to do things
   that he can't quite manage,
   and be pleased when he succeeds.
So may we grow up together
   not just as brothers
   but as life-long friends.

Peter Dainty

The Congregation's Prayer

Heavenly Father, we thank you
   that you welcome little children
   into your family,
   just as Jesus welcomed them
   by holding them in his arms
   and blessing them at his knee.
We thank you that you love them
   before they even know you,
   or can even speak your name.

Help us to show them your love
  by being loving and patient
  towards them ourselves,
  and telling them of Jesus,
  who gave himself in love
  for all the world.
Amen.

Peter Dainty

The Priest's/Minister's Prayer

Loving Father,
   I thank you
   that ...(parents' names)...
   are bringing their baby son
   for baptism today.
May the church truly welcome them
   and rejoice with them
   on this special occasion.
In all the pleasure
   and excitement of the day:

the family gathering,
   the eating and drinking,
   the laughter and conversation,
   may ...(parents' names)... not forget
   that baptism marks
   the beginning of ...(baby's name)...'s
   Christian life
   in the family of God,
   and realise
   the significance of that
   in all the days to come.
Amen.

Peter Dainty

Lord Jesus Christ, our Lord most dear,
as you were once an infant here,
so give this child of yours, we pray,
your grace and blessing day by day.

Their watch let angels round him keep
where'er he be, awake, asleep.
Be pleased your caring love to give,
and keep this child by morn and eve.

As in your heavenly kingdom, Lord,
all things obey your sacred word,
may he your holy cross so bear
that with your saints a crown he'll wear.

Heinrich von Laufenberg (fifteenth century)
trans. Catherine Winkworth (1827-78)

First published in 2004 by

KEVIN MAYHEW LTD
Buxhall, Stowmarket, Suffolk, IP14 3BW
E-mail: info@kevinmayhewltd.com

© 2004 Peter Dainty

9 8 7 6 5 4 3 2 1 0

ISBN 1 84417 344 5
Catalogue No. 1500756

Designed by Angela Selfe
Illustrations by Amanda Smith and Angela Palfrey

Printed and bound in China